British Railway Memories:

No. 81 TYNESIDE ELECT

SOUTH SHIELDS BRANCH & SYSTEM MISCELLANY

David Dunn

INTRODUCTION

Welcome to the second volume of Tyneside Electrics. In this album we feature the South Tyneside line to South Shields, have a look at South Gosforth car sheds, view some associated miscellany, storage of the withdrawn units, the last day workings, and finally the scrapping carried out in North Blyth. Quite a mixture but one which will compliment the images presented in Volume 1.

Both volumes contain enough illustrations to convey our idea of what the Tyneside electric system looked like in the BR period when we actually used it for our daily purposes. We have also included some 'ancient' images from 'the olden days' when most of us were not even born. Enjoy!

David Dunn, Cramlington, March 2016

(cover) See page 4.

(previous page) Before the signals were changed! An eight-car South Shields bound EMU composed of 1920 replacement stock runs off the High Level bridge into Gateshead station circa 1950. Note the neatness of the boarded crossing. *J.W.Armstrong (ARPT)*.

Printed and bound by The Amadeus Press, Cleckheaton, West Yorkshire
First published in the United Kingdom by Book Law Publications, 382 Carlton Hill, Nottingham, NG4 1JA

The new South Tyneside service required thirty-six vehicles formed into eighteen two-car sets. Each set consisted a motor car coupled to a trailer with driving gear. Only nine of the motor cars had luggage facilities. With only thirty-five elliptical roof stock in existence, one luggage motor car was built at York to the same design. The stock was refurbished in 1937-8 and three motor cars were converted into trailers. The electrical equipment was updated, and the reversible seats were replaced by fixed seats.

The new service began on Monday 14th March 1938.

In 1955 BR replaced the elliptical roof stock with new stock to a SR design. The remaining NER stock was withdrawn in 1955; the last recorded service operating was to South Shields on Tuesday 17th May 1955.

The High Level bridge at Newcastle was closed on Sundays from 22nd February to 3rd May 1959 and electric trains on the South Shields line were replaced by DMUs and diverted via King Edward bridge in and out of Newcastle (Central). A reversal was made in and out of the station at Gateshead (West).

6th January 1963 – Electric trains withdrawn from South Shields line.

(above) A six-car formation of original 1904 clerestory roof stock stables at Pelaw station on an unknown date but probably not long after the electrification of the South Shields route.   *J.W.Armstrong (ARPT).*   3

The new electric units for South Shields went into regular service on 10th February 1955, the first train being the 1100 from Newcastle (Central). According to the local newspapers the new trains can do the journey in five minutes less time than before! One of the Eastleigh units on No.6 road outside the car sheds at South Gosforth 12th September 1960. This is E77101 which was twinned with E65312. All the information about the unit is contained in those two nondescript panels on the front of the cab – Tare 30-tons, overall length & width 132ft 8½ins. 9ft 3ins. These units spent just eight years on Tyneside before returning to southern England. A 2-EPB unit from Tyneside also survives in preservation: 1954-built set (cars Nos.65321 and 77112) is owned by the Suburban Electric Railway Association. *L.G.Charlton (ARPT)*.

The 1955 SR Parcels van E68000 at South Gosforth car sheds on 15th April 1960. This was the last of the SR-built stock to reach Tyneside and it was intended to work the South Shields branch. Its arrival was somewhat delayed and in the last week of October 1955 it was reported that E68000 had arrived at Peckham Rye depot SR for a series of tests which included haulage of a 350-ton empty stock train between London and Brighton, and a freight train between Norwood Junction and Three Bridges. However a series of mishaps, fires, loss of vacuum, and even a collision, kept the unit on the SR until December. 'New' ex-Eastleigh, Parcels Van E68000 arrived at South Gosforth car sheds on 3rd January 1956 from SR. The legends on the front face inform us that its weight was 49-tons, length 67ft 1in., width 9ft 3ins. and its last lifted date was 4th October 1955. Note that the vehicle has a normal hook with a buck-eye coupling attached but no screw coupling; the coupling vehicle would provide the necessary. When withdrawn from service on Tyneside, E68000 was transferred to the Liverpool area where it became M68000M.   *N.W.Skinner (ARPT).*

A North Tyneside 1938 stock unit runs a South Tyneside stopping service to South Shields out of platform 6 at Newcastle (Central) circa 1953.

Christopher Campbell.

The more usual fare for the South Tyneside services from platform 6 in 1953 – a 1920 replacement unit with elliptical roof. Those peep holes for the driver never ceased to amaze. Were they adjustable or was it all down to the position of the seat? *Christopher Campbell.* 7

(opposite, top) Before the snow arrived! The junction at Pelaw saw much more traffic than the South Shields electrics coming and going but on this afternoon of Wednesday 19th December 1962 a two-car set runs across from the Hebburn line towards the Pelaw station stop. *(opposite, bottom)* A smattering of snow has fallen overnight! A four-car formation runs across the junction at Pelaw bound for Central on 24th December 1962. *both I.S.Carr (ARPT).*

(above) Displaying the headlight code used for all the Tyneside electric stock but not always discernible in photographs, a four-car formation is passing Pelaw and shows it is on a Central to South Shields service – two upper white lights and no lower lights! *I.S.Carr (ARPT).*

FELLING

NORTH EASTERN RAILWAY
PUBLIC WARNING
PERSONS ARE WARNED NOT TO TRESPASS
ON THIS RAILWAY, OR ON ANY OF THE
LINES, STATIONS, WORKS, OR PREMISES
CONNECTED THEREWITH.
ANY PERSON SO TRESPASSING IS LIABLE
TO A PENALTY OF FORTY SHILLINGS.
R. L WEDGWOOD
SECRETARY

LNER
ELECTRIFICATION
CAUTION
IT IS DANGEROUS
TO TOUCH THE
ELEVATED RAILS

Felling was the next station encountered after Gateshead when travelling eastbound. Alongside the signal box at Felling station on Christmas Eve 1962 stood these rather grand and somewhat historical cast-iron notices which contrast nicely with the BR orange information notice. Now, can anyone give us a reasonable explanation why only some of the first letters of the words making up the public warning were twice the size of the rest? The signage related to the electrification on the south side of the Tyne was all LNER whereas that on the north side was North Eastern Railway.

I.S.Carr (ARPT).

(above) A Christmas card scene at Pelaw in late 1962 as a two-car 2-EPB calls whilst en route to South Shields. *(below)* At about the same time in late December 1962, a Newcastle bound unit calls at Pelaw. The destination blind shows South Shields so that was never changed as long as the unit remained on the out and back working facing that way. In the great scheme, the guards compartment always faced Newcastle, or though it seemed.

both E.Wilson (ARPT).

Bound for Newcastle, what appears to be a six-car formation of 1920 stock runs off the South Shields branch at Pelaw in February 1952; these units still had a couple more years' service before the arrival of the BR units from the Southern Region workshops.   *E.Wilson (ARPT).*

South Shields, Saturday 3rd June 1950 and a view from the River Drive overbridge reveals 1920 elliptical roof stock car E23212, a Single Driving Motor-3rd unit stabled at the end of the branch with others of its ilk. Note BRITISH RAILWAYS adorns the end of the vehicle whilst the E prefix is half the size of the figures. A sister set is stabled on the adjacent track but that unit retains – for now – the LNER lozenge motif in the centre of the car. All of these units were replacements for those lost in the fire at Heaton in 1918. Displaced from the North Tyneside electrified lines by the new Metro-Camm units in 1938, these 1920 NER replacement vehicles were modernised in 1938 to take on the work on the newly electrified South Shields line. Some 35 vehicles were involved in the changeover (York built a 36th in 1938 to even out the distribution of motors and trailers). E23212 became E29175E and was withdrawn in 1955 with the introduction of the BR(SR) stock. Livery in this 1950 image is blue and grey. The first South Tyneside stock withdrawal took place in May 1941 when Diagram 220 Trailer No.23249 was damaged beyond repair in a German air raid on South Shields. For the record, the first withdrawal of any of the Tyneside 1938 stock was set No.24229 and 24230 which were destroyed by German incendiary bombs which hit Monkseaton carriage sidings in the early hours of Thursday 10th April 1941. The set was withdrawn a few months later at Gosforth Car Sheds. That bombing raid during the night of 9th and 10th April involved seventy German bombers which dropped many thousands of incendiary bombs on Tyneside causing widespread damage; the human casualties that night included thirty-three dead and countless dozens injured! This morning view of the Tyne in the immediate post-war period depicts much of what was and much of what no longer exists. Shipping of all shapes and sizes are berthed two and three deep at yards lining the banks where building and/or repair was being undertaken.   *L.G.Charlton (ARPT)*.

E29183E and E29383E, with 26500, stable at South Gosforth on 16th March 1955 after withdrawal from the South Shields services. This car once had two driving positions but the nearest was removed to make this strange combination with the destination indicator inside the unit.
L.G.Charlton (ARPT).

(opposite) On a date yet to be established, one of the Eastleigh-built units consisting six cars crosses the High Level bridge as it strides out to South Shields. The droplight windows in each of the slam doors have come into their own on these units, the absence of sliding doors required a new method of ventilating the passenger saloons in these new cars during the warmer months.
J.W.Armstrong (ARPT).

Early days on the South Tyneside route as a six-car train of 1920 replacement stock approach Central off the High Level bridge with a service from South Shields. Note the driver's small cut-out observation window with a face just visible. It is also worth noting the number of open sliding doors which would constitute danger under any regime! There was some interesting trackwork within and just beyond the crossing.
E.R.Wethersett, M.Halbert collection.

(opposite, top) An ex NER unit working the South Shields services at Central on the afternoon of Tuesday 29th June 1954. The days of these 1920 replacement units were numbered as new BR stock in the shape of SR units was just months away from arriving on Tyneside. *(opposite, bottom)* Standing in platform 6 in virtually the same spot as the NER unit illustrated above, one of the new SR Eastleigh modified 2-EPB units works a South Tyneside service on 12th March 1955. These sets were still being delivered at this time but early April would see all fifteen of the twin-units resident on Tyneside. The changes made to suit local requirements included enlarging the guard's and luggage van, necessitating one less seating bay in the motor car, and the inclusion of a 1st class compartment in the trailer.
both F.W.Hampson (ARPT).

18   A six-car formation of 1938 stock traverses the HLB with a South Shields service pre-1955.   *J.W.Armstrong (ARPT).*

Some years later one of the SR units consisting four cars heads into Gateshead station with a South Shields service circa 1958. Note that the semaphores have been replaced by colour-light signals.

J.W.Armstrong (ARPT). 19

(above) An eight-car North Tyneside unit – with Type A DMT E29104E leading – works the South Shields branch on Wednesday 9th April 1958 and was photographed beneath the signal gantry at Pelaw. *W.R.E.Lewis (ARPT).*

(opposite) Gateshead Park Lane as seen from the compartment of an Eastleigh-built EMU on the 30th December 1962. The winter had only just started and these 2-EPBs were having none of it. *I.S.Carr (ARPT)*. It was reported in September 1960 that trials over the Tyneside electrified lines with diesel railcars have again been held. The LNER articulated stock on the North Tyneside line is said to be due for renewal shortly, and there has been talk of abandoning electrification! Derby-built 3-car DMU set M51861, M51862, and M59725 was in normal traffic on Wednesday 7th and Thursday 8th September and managed to keep time. On Friday 9th September trials were held on the South Tyneside line between Newcastle and South Shields. Two years passed before further rumours in October 1962 stated that the South Tyneside electric service would cease early in the New Year and be replaced by diesel units. Sunday 6th January 1963 – The last electric train between Newcastle (Central) and South Shields ran on this day, and next day DMUs took over. By 9th January the third rail had been lifted over High Level Bridge and at least ten electric cars had left for the SR. Parcels trains are now steam worked by V3s from Heaton and No.67652 was noted on 7th January. It was November and December 1963 before many of the former Tyneside 2-EPBs were fully operational on the SR again and the last batch – S65311/15/18 and S77100/04/07 were not added to SR stock until 11th August 1964, some twenty months after they ceased working the South Tyneside services.

above) A South Shields-Newcastle service runs into Pelaw circa 1952. *R.F.Payne (ARPT). (below)* An unidentified unit at Pelaw on a seasonal 27th December 1962. *I.S.Carr (ARPT).*

This is Tyne Dock station on 16th September 1962 with another unidentified 2-EPB.

I.S.Carr (ARPT). 23

A two-car EMU departs from Tyne Dock station circa 1962. On the right is one of the colliery lines which proliferate around this part of the North-
East.

I.S.Carr (ARPT).

above) Sporting a yellow warning panel, an unidentified 2-EPB departs from High Shields and heads for Newcastle on 6th December 1962. *(below)* On that same afternoon a South Shields service gets ready to depart High Shields on the last leg of its journey. *both Christopher Campbell.*

A rather dirty two-car unit departs from South Shields in January 1963. The snow is sparse but the cold was relentless and temperatures plunged for weeks on end. These electric units managed to bring a modicum of comfort and warmth for the weary traveller; simply commuting could be fraught with discomfort, and sometimes danger. Now, that roof looks fit enough to handle any amount of snow.   *J.W.Armstrong (ARPT).*

A Metro-Camm DMU meets a 2-EPB EMU (E77106) at South Shields during the winter of 1962. The diesel was working a service to Sunderland but plans were being made ready for the take-over in the summer of 1963 and similar diesel units were already running certain services from Central.

J.W.Armstrong (ARPT). 27

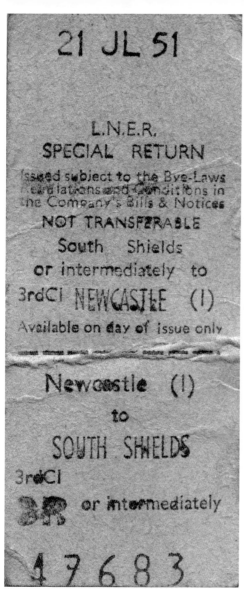

21 JL 51

L.N.E.R.
SPECIAL RETURN
Issued subject to the Bye-Laws
Regulations and Conditions in
the Company's Bills & Notices
NOT TRANSFERABLE
South   Shields
or intermediately to
3rdCl NEWCASTLE (I)
Available on day of issue only

Newcastle (I)
to
SOUTH SHIELDS
3rdCl
BR   or intermediately

47683

above left) On a dark and chilly 5th January 1963 2-EPB E65322E waits for departure at South Shields with a Newcastle service. Again the two lights at the top with none below depict the service.
I.S.Carr (ARPT).
An LNER Special Return 3rd Class ticket from South Shields to Newcastle (Central). Issued 21st July 1951!   *Christopher Campbell coll.*

(above) Making for South Shields, E68000 runs across the junction at Pelaw with a couple of vans in tow. A lightweight load compared with some of the test trains it hauled whilst Eastleigh appraised its capabilities. We have no date but the low winter midday sun and frost covering the ground on the left would bring us to winter at a guess! *D.R.Dunn coll.* *(below)* A six-car BR Standard EMU stables at Pelaw circa 1962. Note that not all the guard's compartments are at the Newcastle end of each unit. Whereas the to and froing between South Shields and Newcastle could virtually guarantee to keep the units in a particular formation, the coming and going to the car sheds at South Gosforth would eventually take its toll on any standardisation of formation positions! *R.F.Payne (ARPT).*

MISCELLANY

(above & below) The surviving fifteen passenger cars that were built between 1909 and 1915 were used for workmen's' trains for a couple of years although from 1940 to 1945 they were stored with other redundant cars as possible replacements in the event of air-raid damage; they were never required and in 1945 were cut up. During that period, the fifteen cars were distributed amongst the engine sheds at Darlington, Scarborough, Staveley, and Thirsk. Here at the S&D crossing in Darlington fourteen of those same cars are stored alongside the main line. Their place of destruction after the conflict is unknown.   *J.W.Armstrong (ARPT).*

A NER self explanatory sign. *Ian Spencer.*

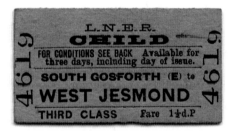

(right) A January 1933 LNER notice advertising Cheap Workmen's Tickets on the North Tyneside lines. Both stop/start timings and fares are illustrated to give us a flavour of social history some eighty-odd years ago.

Mark Williams coll.

CHEAP WORKMEN'S TICKETS
ARE ISSUED FROM
BLYTH NEWSHAM & HARTLEY
TO
NORTH SHIELDS HOWDON
WALLSEND & NEWCASTLE

AVAILABLE BY THE FOLLOWING TRAINS

	Weekdays		*
	am	am	am
BLYTH............dep	6 30	7 30	7 50
NEWSHAM .... ,,	6 36	7 36	8 2
HARTLEY .... ,,	6 40	7 40	8 7
MONKSEATON......arr	6 48	7 48	...
......,, ...dep	6 58	7 57	...
NORTH SHIELDS ...arr	7 10	8 9	...
HOWDON .... ,,	7 17	8†22	...
WALLSEND .... ,,	7 21	8 19	...
NEWCASTLE (Central) ,,	7 33	8 32	...
,, (Manors N) ,,			8 41

† Passengers for Howden depart Monkseaton at 8-3 am

	Mondays to Fridays inclusive		Sats only		Weds only
	pm	pm	pm	pm	pm
NEWCASTLE ....dep		5 25	12 25	1 25	1 22
MANORS NORTH ... ,,	5*24	...	...	...	1 24
WALLSEND ,,	...	5 26	12 26	1 26	..
HOWDON ,,	...	5 30	12 30	1 30	...
NORTH SHIELDS ,,	...	5 36	12 36	1 36	...
MONKSEATON......arr	...	5 48	12 48	1 48	..
MONKSEATON......arr	...	5 53	12 53	1 53	..
,, ...dep	...	6 5	12 58	1 58	..
HARTLEY ....arr	...	6 13	1 6	2 6	1 53
NEWSHAM .... ,,	5*52	6 18	1 11	2 11	1 57
BLYTH............ ,,	5*59	6 22	1 15	2 15	2 7

* Via Seghill

In addition to above trains workmen are allowed to return by any train after 5-0 pm, except the 5-40 pm ex Central and 5-42 pm ex Manors

FARES
WORKMEN'S TICKETS are issued as follows :—

FROM	TO	Daily Tickets	Weekly Sets
BLYTH ....NEWCASTLE		11d	5/3
NEWSHAM .... ,,		11d	5/3
HARTLEY .... ,,		10½d	5/-
BLYTH ....NO SHIELDS		10d	....
,, ...HOWDON		11d	....
,, ...WALLSEND		1/-	....

For further information apply to the District Passenger Manager at Newcastle Tel 20741
FOR CONDITIONS OF ISSUE SEE OTHER SIDE

NEWCASTLE Jan 1933

L·N·E·R

HN 245—Howe Bros Gateshead—250

WORKMEN'S TICKETS

North Shields etc. to Backworth Benton & South Gosforth

Available by following trains—

OUTWARD (Weekdays)		am	am	am	am	RETURN (Weekdays, Weds and Sats excepted)					pm		
North Shields	... dep	6 41	7 11	7 41	8 11	South Gosforth	... dep	4 36	...				
Tynemouth	... „	6 44	7 14	7 44	8 14	Benton	... „	4 40	...			And
Cullercoats	... „	6 48	7 18	7 48	8 18	Backworth	... „	4 46	...			all
Whitley Bay	... „	6 50	7 20	7 50	8 20	Monkseaton	... arr	4 53	...			slow
Monkseaton	... „	6 53	7 23	7 53	8 23	Whitley Bay	... „	4 56	...			trains
Backworth	... arr	7 1	7 31	8 1	8 31	Cullercoats	... „	4 58	...			after-
Benton	... „	7 7	7 37	8 7	8 37	Tynemouth	... „	5 1	...			wards
South Gosforth	... „	7 11	7 41	8 11	8 41	North Shields	... „	5 5	...			

RETURN (Wednesdays and Saturdays only)

		pm	pm	pm	pm	pm	pm			
South Gosforth	... dep	12 16	12 36	12 56	1 16	1 36	4 36	...	...	And
Benton	... „	12 20	12 40	1 0	1 20	1 40	4 40	...	...	all
Backworth	... „	12 26	12 46	1 6	1 26	1 46	4 46	...	...	slow
Monkseaton	... arr	12 33	12 53	1 13	1 33	1 53	4 53	...	...	trains
Whitley Bay	... „	12 36	12 56	1 16	1 36	1 56	4 56	...	...	after-
Cullercoats	... „	12 38	12 58	1 18	1 38	1 58	4 56	...	...	wards
Tynemouth	... „	12 41	1 1	1 21	1 41	2 1	5 1	...	...	
North Shields	... „	12 45	1 5	1 25	1 45	2 5	5 5	...	...	

FARES

From	Backworth Daily	Weekly	Benton Daily	Weekly	South Gosforth Daily	Weekly
North Shields	7d.	3/6	8½d.	4/3	10d.	—
Tynemouth	6d.	3/-	—	—	—	—
Cullercoats	—	—	—	—	8d.	—
Whitley Bay	4½d.	2/3	6½d.	3/3	—	—
Monkseaton	—	—	6d.	3/-	—	—
Backworth	—	—	—	—	5½d.	2/9

FOR CONDITIONS OF ISSUE SEE OTHER SIDE

For further information apply to District Passenger Manager, Newcastle, Tel 20741.

YORK, Sept., 1936.　　L·N·E·R　　Herald, York—1,000

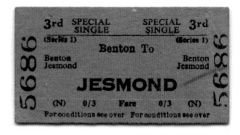

(left) This Workmen's Ticket's notice dates from September 1936.　　*Author's collection.*

Newcastle (Central) had seen a number of accidents involving the Tyneside electric stock over the years. One of the last to occur, in January 1959, involved this unit which collided head-on with an empty unit which was being shunted. The driver of the incoming train sadly lost his life. In another, but far more catastrophic, incident Driving Trailer No.29312 and Driving Motor No.29131 collided at Newcastle Central on Friday 17th August 1951, and as a result they were withdrawn. The surviving halves of these two sets (Motor Third No.29112 and Trailer Third No.29231) were united to form a new twin set. No.29112 was renumbered as No.29131 for consistency with the numbering system being used. However, that accident had numerous human casualties too. It was found that the August 1951 accident was primarily caused by driver error. There were three fatalities and some forty-one people were injured. The 1035 train from Newcastle to Newcastle via the Wallsend circular started from No.2 terminal platform at Central with the signal at danger; after travelling just 36 yards it collided almost head-on at a slip connection with the 0935 train from Newcastle to Newcastle via Benton which was entering No.1 platform under clear signals. The combined speed of the trains was about 25 m.p.h. The left side of the leading coach of each train was torn away. The incoming train was due into platform 1 at 1028 but was running seven or eight minutes late. The Motorman of the incoming train and a passenger in its leading coach were killed whilst another passenger died in hospital. Nineteen passengers were conveyed to hospital of which eight were detained. A further twenty passengers were treated for shock and minor injuries. The Motorman and guard of the outgoing train were also injured but allowed home after treatment.

F.W.Hampson (ARPT).

(opposite) Just in case you have forgotten what the eastern end of Central station looked like, here it is circa 1964 from that well known vantage point – The Keep! A couple of Gresley A3s equipped with trough-like smoke deflectors have come over from Gateshead shed and are ready to take on northbound trains. Behind them a B1 with a clean smokebox front also awaits employment. Departing platform 2 is a six-car North Tyneside unit passing the shunter pilot and a BR Sulzer Type 2. Nothing has changed from the last time we looked. Now then, wouldn't it be nice to see a 4mm model of that junction? A challenge? Go on then, and don't forget that double catch point either! *Malcolm Dunnett (ARPT).*

(above) Now here is a nice surprise! Clayton Type 1 D8594 was captured on film running back to Newcastle with Parcels Van E29467E after the electric unit had been seconded in the event of their being no locomotive hauled stock available for a regular working which took the locomotive and stock to Durham and back. The date is 17th June 1967 and the location is the East Coast Main line at Lamesley at sometime in the late morning. Now some might say this was pure co-incidence, being the last day and all, but to see a Clayton with a clean exhaust actually hauling something really was a scoop for the photographer! Such an incidence was never recorded again. *Trevor Ermel.*

Ex-MPV 3267 in its later guise as a de-icing van and numbered DE 900730. Now part of the National collection but look at it stabled/stored/dumped at Monkwearmouth on 24th May 1977! Note that the vehicle still retains the de-icing equipment which can be seen attached to the nearest bogie with the two feed lines running out of the rear compartment. It would be interesting to know just how much of the preserved vehicle is original, and in what guise it has been saved for the nation.

I.S.Carr (ARPT).

SOUTH GOSFORTH

South Gosforth Motive Power Depot – or should that be Car Sheds? – on 29th September 1963 with the two ES1s Nos.26500 and 26501 both resplendent in lined NER green livery. The pair were, by now, sixty-one years old. 29th February 1964 – the two Class ES1 electric shunting locomotives 26500 and 26501 were withdrawn and a 350 h.p. 0-6-0DE shunter took over on the Quayside branch from Monday 2nd March. Electric and diesel units share the car sheds, which were no longer the domain of the Tyneside electric units. A six-road extension was planned to be built here in the late 1950s for the maintenance of the DMUs, a sign that they were here to stay. Eventually the diesels took over; the gradual decline of electric workings on the Tyneside system began shortly after the SR-built two-car units arrived from Eastleigh. *F.W.Hampson (ARPT).*

(opposite, top) South Gosforth on 1st May 1962 with Derby Lightweight DMUs making their mark amongst the other DMUs. Note that the third-rail is everywhere which required vigilance the whole time. *D.J.Dippie. (opposite, bottom)* Two Parcels/Luggage vans from very different eras at South Gosforth 1st April 1956 with the clean modern lines of virtually new E68000 contrasts greatly with the all timber construction of E29493E. From this angle it appears that the older vehicle has been involved in one of those heavy shunting accidents which tend to bend the frames of the victims. *F.W.Hampson (ARPT).*

(above) South Gosforth depot and workshops from the east end on 8th April 1951. To the right of the car sheds the land belonged to the Boy Scout Association i.e. The 51st Newcastle in which yours truly was a Patrol Leader!! *F.W.Hampson (ARPT).*

Two perambulator cars at the rear of South Gosforth car sheds on 11th September 1960. Their short season was virtually finished but another year of use might be in the offing. Powerless, and virtually useless for any other purpose, the pair were lucky to survive each winter storage. *L.G.Charlton (ARPT). (opposite)* Photographer L.G.Charlton stands on the top step of ES1 No.26500 before stepping into the cab at South Gosforth car sheds on Sunday 11th September 1960. The light and airy interior of the sheds was a distinct opposite to those other motive power buildings, the engine shed. However, the exterior condition of the little Bo-Bo leaves a lot to be desired and it has a similar finish to most steam locomotives of that period. Before we leave this somewhat sterile atmosphere, it is worth commenting on the method of moving these locomotives and units about the shed when no apparent means of power – conductor rail or overhead catenary – was available. In actuality overhead power was available but in a more domestic style of delivery; the thick insulated wire hanging down from the roof near the front of 26500, was in fact a power source with two plugs which could be connected to the units to move them along the road either way. The top of the wire was connected to a small four-wheel bogie which ran on two wires for the length of the workshop. Every two roads was supplied with a power source. 26500 and sister used their pantographs and the overhead.

L.G.Charlton collection. 41

RUN-DOWN - Withdrawals of the regular stock began in 1963 when there was a drastic reduction in the North Tyneside services – fifteen two-car units were condemned. These initial withdrawals were of two-car units with only one cab, those units with two cabs allowed for more flexible operating and were kept in work. The situation by the end of 1966 saw the following still operational: Type A – 11 twins; Type B – 16 twins; Type C – 6 twins; Type D – 14 twins. Withdrawal of these remaining cars was started in spring 1967; the last service ran on 17th June 1967. These were the last examples of articulated LNER stock in operation on BR. However, we must go back to December 1958 to see where BR had started the gradual transition from electric to diesel on the North Tyneside electrified lines: For two weeks commencing Monday 1st December 1958, diesel multiple units replaced some of the electric units on the North Tyneside line during peak periods. The use of these diesel units was experimental to determine working conditions over the route, costs and timekeeping. On Mondays to Fridays seven electric trains working Newcastle to Newcastle via Tynemouth were replaced, together with four trains on Saturdays. Withdrawal of electric services on the North Tyneside lines was scheduled to take place from 3rd June 1967 onwards but availability of sufficient diesel units saw BR cancelling that event for two weeks until 17th June 1967. Although about half the trains were run by DMUs, more than thirty-two twin units of the 1938 stock was still working during the week commencing Saturday 3rd June 1967.

In April 1964 it was further reported that – Since the introduction of the winter timetable, all off-peak trains on the North Tyneside electric services now consist of two cars only, and at least sixteen twin-units of the 1936 stock are now stored in Heaton goods yard. It is proposed to withdraw the trains on the Riverside loop in June 64' but this may be postponed for a while because of the lack of other means of transport for the many shipyard workers who use the trains. Consideration is also being given to the possible abandonment of electrification in September and replacement by DMUs. To allow for the additional running times, an extra five minutes has already been added to the schedules of stopping trains between Newcastle and Newcastle via Tynemouth in both directions to enable diesels to be used.

(above) E29468E again but this time at South Gosforth after the closure. Sister E29467E in a similar state of distress is stabled behind. *E.Wilson (ARPT). (opposite)* Withdrawn units stored at the east end of Heaton shed. The shed here had been abandoned when steam was officially evicted in June 1963 but gradually the steam locomotives crept back to use the repair facilities, and to be stored. Diesel locomotives also used the depot for refuelling, especially those collecting or depositing carriage stock in the nearby siding. Naturally the eight shed roads attracted the redundant articulated electric units during the latter operational days of the North Tyneside system as here; South Gosforth could only house so many of the laid-off units and the daily working of the depot could not be compromised by withdrawn or stored stock cluttering the sidings. Numbers recorded included NE29120E, E29315E, and E29316E with their matching sets; all Type B! Note the Hebburn destination displayed on the centre unit. *I.S.Carr (ARPT).* 43

Units were stored in the most unlikely of places. The Heaton coaling stage had however been redundant for nearly four years when this image was recorded on 9th April 1967.

Ken Groundwater (ARPT).

Another image from Heaton on 9th April 1967 with abandonment being the order of the day. Even the roller blind indicators have got in on the act displaying Newcastle – Empty Train. This is E29309E, one of that month's condemnations!   *K.Groundwater (ARPT).*

It wasn't even the last day! Ten cars are crammed into this siding at Heaton MPD on 9th April 1967. In January 1960 the first Tyneside unit to be painted in the new dark green livery – E29159E+E29259E – emerged from overhaul at Walker Gate shops. Was it only seven years ago? According to the legend on the end panel, this car was painted green in January 1962 during a major overhaul.   *K.Groundwater (ARPT).*

Here is an earlier occupant of the sidings at Heaton although these are the carriage sidings. Old timer DE90733 which was a one-time luggage and parcels van but latterly in use as a sleet van awaits its demise at Heaton on Saturday 24th April 1954.   *F.W.Hampson (ARPT).*

Type C E29238E and DMBT E29166E stored at Monkseaton car sidings on 3rd March 1967. Both vehicles have been relieved of their electrical pick-up gear and supporting beam but neither had yet been withdrawn. The inevitable happened in April and May respectively.   *I.S.Carr (ARPT)*.

Another aspect of the EMU storage at Monkseaton on 3rd March 67' where an eight car set has joined the DMBT.   *I.S.Carr (ARPT).*   49

THE LAST DAY

(above) The last Tyneside electric service ran on 17th June 1967 and consisted an eight-car set to work the 1815 Newcastle – Wallsend – Tynemouth – Benton – Newcastle. This is part of the 'crush' trying to board the train at Central, the bemused commuters wondering why all those enthusiasts had suddenly materialised to join the train. Where were you? *Trevor Ermel. (right)* Not a Last day ticket but one from 1956 allowing the passenger one-way passage for the sum of 2d – less than one pence! Later schemes were run to attract more passengers to the off-peak trains but they, alas, failed too!

Christopher Campbell coll.

Central's concourse in the area of platforms 3 & 4 on that last day. The last electric train (to the coast via Wallsend) is advertised as though it was just an excursion or a football special – nothing fancy, no razzmatazz, no hype – lets get it over and done with, its clapped out so its got to go! The ticket inspector appeals to the photographer to hurry along or you won't be getting aboard! *Kevin Hudspith.* 51

(left) The front end of that last day, last electric train, 1815 hrs 17th June 1967 departure. *(right)* Later into the journey, the driver of that last day Newcastle to Newcastle via Wallsend service.

both K.Groundwater (ARPT).

Cullercoats station on the last day as viewed from the sharp end. The original station dated from 1864 but this station was re-sited on the deviation in July 1882. Closing from Monday 10th September 1979 for conversion to a Metro station, Cullercoats re-opened for business on Monday 11th August 1980.

K.Groundwater (ARPT).

54   The north end of Cullercoats – as seen from the cab of that last train on the evening of 17th June 1967.   *K.Groundwater (ARPT).*

Running beneath one of the bridges carrying the Backworth system colliery railway down to Percy Main, the last day service approaches the junction at Backworth where the B&T heads north to Blyth.   *K.Groundwater (ARPT).*

The view from the embankment towards the junction as a two-car unit from Monkseaton approaches Backworth. This wasn't the last day but it was early 1967. Note the new signal box.

K.Gregory (ARPT).

Traversing beneath the road bridge carrying the B1322, we enter Backworth station from the east. If we treat the North Tyneside loop as just that, we are travelling in an anticlockwise direction. In front of us another Backworth system colliery line spans the station just where the platforms straighten out. Opened by the North Eastern Railway in late June 1864, to replace another nearby station located on the B&T system and known as Holywell, this new station was initially called Hotspur but was renamed Backworth in the following year. Closed on 13th June 1977, the station was not one of those converted for the T&W Metro.   *K.Groundwater (ARPT).*

Longbenton station as viewed from the last electric train on the last day. This station was the newest on the line, if not the whole of Tyneside. Opened 14th July 1947 by the LNER – primarily for the opening of the new Ministry of Pensions & National Insurance buildings – the design is pure post-war austere with brick and concrete being the main components in its construction. Closed 23rd January 1978 for conversion to a Metro station, the station opened for business again on 11th August 1980 and is still thriving. In 1964 a BR service train left the Car Sheds at 0510 to Benton thence to Newcastle for BR employees. It was used by shift workers at the cost of a tanner (6d), the equivalent of two and a half new pence, paid to the Ticket Collectors Benevolent Society!

Trevor Ermel.

That last train returns to Central on the evening of Saturday 17th June 1967. No fanfare, pomp or circumstance! *K.Groundwater (ARPT).* 59

Parcels Van E29467E stabled out of the way on the south side of Central station on that last day, 17th June 1967. This must have been after its foray
with the Clayton earlier in the day for it is now late evening.   *I.S.Carr (ARPT)*.

STORAGE AFTER THE LAST DAY

The west end of the 'redundant' engine shed at Heaton on 2nd July 1967. Three years previously it was announced that '...since the winter timetable of 1963-64 was introduced, all off-peak trains consisted two-cars only and as a consequence some sixteen twin units of the 1938 stock were stored at Heaton goods yard from that date...' Those early withdrawals were destined for North Blyth and were soon in the hands of Hughes Bolckow with images of their storage at Heaton goods rather rare; not so the summer 1967 lot! Some of this latest batch were also destined for the Blyth scrapyard but quite a number apparently ended their days in Scotland!   *Ken Groundwater (ARPT).*

(above) Two Type B units, E29316E, on the right, and NE29120E, nearest, languish outside the east end of an equally derelict Heaton engine shed on Sunday 2nd July 1967. Both of these units worked up to the final day and note that one of them carried the latest in regional designations. The addition of the NE prefix seems with hindsight – and probably at the time to many – to have been a total waste of time especially as the North Eastern Region of BR had recently been amalgamated with the Eastern Region to form one region which now stretched from London to the Scottish border. Anyway, for enthusiasts it was another diversion and besides, photographs of these 'renumberings' are quite rare. *K.Groundwater (ARPT).*

(Opposite) NE29120E again, just to silence any doubters! *K.Groundwater (ARPT).*

(above) Another aspect of the Heaton storage on 2ⁿᵈ July 1967. Diesel locomotives continued to use the fuelling facilities long after the electrics had been hauled away to oblivion. *(left)* Close-up for the modellers: note those wooden window frames!

both K. Groundwater (ARPT).

(left) A saloon seat. *(right)* A vestibule seat! All the passenger doors were manually operated sliding doors. *both K.Groundwater (ARPT).*

Motor Parcels Van E29468E (Whitley Bay is showing on the destination blind) and others – including Type D E29264E & E29164E – are stored at Heaton on 21st July 1968. Note also the redundant Derby Lightweight diesel multiple units joining the throng. *I.S.Carr (ARPT)*.

Storage became a problem initially after the electric services were finally curtailed and a lot of units were stored away from the parent system. At least six decommissioned articulated units were stored alongside the branch at Callerton near Ponteland awaiting their fate in 1967. The station here opened in June 1905 and closed in June 1929 but coal traffic kept the branch open.

E.Wilson (ARPT). 67

SCRAP

One of the Perambulator cars which had long been out of service and was being used as a mess room – equipped with a coal burning stove and a
68 mystery bracket on the roof between the middle door and the end – at an unknown location which was possibly Shildon.   *J.W.Armstrong (ARPT).*

Type C E29236E and E29136E dumped in the Hughes Bolckow yard at North Blyth on 13th July 1967. These two had been withdrawn during the previous April so did not glory in any of the last day celebrations! Others had gone before them and others were yet to arrive here. In November 1964 it was reported that many withdrawn articulated sets previously stored at Heaton had apparently gone to Hughes, Bolckow of North Blyth for scrap! But, on Tuesday 12th January 1965 Gresley V2 No.60931 (St Margarets) left South Gosforth and headed in the Carlisle direction hauling the two unidentified motor coaches and twin units E29150E+E29250E, E29154E+29254E, E29155E+E29255E, E29162E+E29262E (all Type D vehicles withdrawn in June 1964) en route to G.H.Campbell, Shieldhall. It was reported in April 1968 that fifty condemned Tyneside e.m.u. coaches have been sold to J.N.Connel of Coatbridge and that fourteen of the vehicles had been delivered to their yard on 6th February 1968. Fifty appears to be a rather large number still in existence at this late date but some ninety-odd vehicles survived into July 1967 and HB at Blyth did not take them all.

I.S.Carr (ARPT).

(above) Where are those motors? Destruction at Hughes Bolckows in North Blyth during August 1967. *Roy Stevens (ARPT)*. *(below)* One of the June 1964 withdrawals and still very much intact, Type C car E29235E endures its last winter at Hughes Bolckow on Sunday 3rd January 1965. *W.P.Hodgson*.

(above) Seats, side panels, roof panels, broken glass and not much else make up the average North Tyneside electric car. Oh, and those underframes, bogies and motors. I wonder who had those seats and their cushions? Hughes Bolckow 1967. *Trevor Ermel. (below)* Baggage Car M68000M aka E68000 returned to the North-East in 1966 for Willoughbys of Choppington to break up. An inglorious end! *D.R.Dunn coll.*

(above) Four cars await the wreckers in North Blyth in 1967. *(below)* Type D E29257E, withdrawn in April 1967, languishes at Hughes Bolckow later that year.   *both D.R.Dunn coll.*

Epilogue: None of the 1938 cars were preserved, not even, as far as we know, as a cricket pavilion, summer house, chicken shed, pigeon coop, stable, pig sty… DD, 2016.